Organisation of
Political Parties

Researched and written by Reference Services, Central Office of Information.

ISBN 0 11 701838 4

HMSO publications are available from:

HMSO Publications Centre
(Mail, fax and telephone orders only)
PO Box 276, London SW8 5DT
Telephone orders 071-873 9090
General enquiries 071-873 0011
(queuing system in operation for both numbers)
Fax orders 071-873 8200

HMSO Bookshops
49 High Holborn, London WC1V 6HB   071-873 0011
Fax 071-873 8200 (counter service only)
258 Broad Street, Birmingham B1 2HE   021-643 3740   Fax 021-643 6510
Southey House, 33 Wine Street, Bristol BS1 2BQ
0272 264306   Fax 0272 294515
9-21 Princess Street, Manchester M60 8AS   061-834 7201   Fax 061-833 0634
16 Arthur Street, Belfast BT1 4GD   0232 238451   Fax 0232 235401
71 Lothian Road, Edinburgh EH3 9AZ   031-228 4181   Fax 031-229 2734

HMSO's Accredited Agents
(see Yellow Pages)

and through good booksellers

Contents

Introduction

The British[1] system of parliamentary democracy is based on the party system, in which office is sought by organised political parties able to form and support a stable government. The party system itself rests on the assumption that there are at least two parties in the House of Commons, each sufficiently united on matters of policy and principle to be able to form a government at any time. The parties are not registered or formally recognised in law, but in practice most candidates in elections, and almost all winning candidates, belong to one of the main political parties.

After a brief historical background of the origins of the major parties represented in Parliament and an outline of the modern party system, this book describes the organisation—both inside and outside Parliament—of the Conservative, Labour and Liberal Democrat parties. The organisation of the two nationalist parties—the Scottish National Party and Plaid Cymru (Welsh Nationalist Party)—and that of the main political parties in Northern Ireland—Ulster Unionist, Democratic Unionist and Social Democratic and Labour (SDLP)—is considered in separate chapters.

[1] The term 'Britain' is used in this book to mean the United Kingdom of Great Britain and Northern Ireland. 'Great Britain' comprises England, Wales and Scotland.

Historical Background

For over 150 years British parliamentary democracy has been based on a predominantly two-party system: with first Whigs and Tories, then Liberals and Conservatives, and most recently Labour and Conservatives alternating in power.

Associations of like-minded people inevitably arise in any organised society when the principles and practices of government are open to public debate and discussion. In England they have existed in one form or another at least since medieval times. Yet for centuries, and long after the real power in the State had passed from the Crown to Parliament, such associations were loosely knit and short lived. They were usually formed to achieve some particular purpose, and afterwards came to an end, perhaps regrouping for some other cause. The origins of organised political parties in Britain are comparatively recent. Before 1832—the date of the first parliamentary Reform Act—there was no clear-cut division in the House of Commons along modern party lines. The terms 'Whig' and 'Tory' had been in use for about 150 years to describe certain political leanings, but there was no party organisation of any sort outside Parliament. Even within Parliament no strong party discipline existed.

The reason for this lack of organisation lay, to a great extent, in the comparatively small size and exclusive nature of the electorate. In 1830 there were 656 Members of Parliament (MPs) in the House of Commons, slightly more than there are today, but they were returned by an electorate of only about 500,000 out of a total adult population of some 10 million. Many of the growing industrial areas were not represented in Parliament, while ancient country towns sometimes sent two members. The outcome of elections was decided by a small number of influential citizens, and not by the public at large. The personal influence of a candidate counted for more than the policy of a party, and, once elected, an MP did not have to follow a party line.

The growth of the modern party system was brought about by parliamentary reform and the gradual extension of voting rights to the whole adult population. Corrupt election practices were gradually brought to an end, representation in Parliament became more fairly distributed throughout the country, and the social composition of the electorate changed. As a result it became difficult for candidates to offer themselves as individuals to the voters. Politicians, as the representatives of millions of voters able to take part in elections for the first time, began to form organised parties promising to carry out policies which their supporters were prepared to endorse.

Establishment of National Party Organisations

In these circumstances it became obvious that some form of political organisation outside Parliament, as well as within it, was essential if votes were to be won and support maintained. The first organised political parties on the modern pattern—the Conservative and Liberal parties—were, broadly speaking, successors to the Tories and Whigs of the eighteenth and early nineteenth centuries. The word 'Conservative' in its modern political sense first came into use after about 1830 and gradually became a normal expression to describe the successors of the Tories. The Liberal Party was formed towards the end of the 1850s with the support of former Whigs and other political groups.

Both the Liberals and the Conservatives created national headquarters in the 1860s. The Liberal Party central organisation began in 1860 when some Liberal MPs established the Liberal Registration Association, designed to encourage the registration of voters and the growth of constituency associations. Further steps to strengthen Liberal organisations came after a heavy defeat of the Party in the 1874 General Election. In 1877 a large meeting in Birmingham (then the centre of Joseph Chamberlain's successful Liberal association) established the National Liberal Federation, with the aim of forming Liberal constituency associations. Under the Federation's rules, affiliated associations could send representatives to an annual meeting of the Federation's council, a forerunner of the annual party conference.

The Conservative Party, whose full title is the Conservative and Unionist Party, founded the National Union of Conservative and Constitutional Associations in 1867, the year of the second Reform Act, which considerably enlarged the number of voters able to take part in a parliamentary election. The National Union became the national organisation of the Conservative constituency associations, designed to increase popular support for the party outside Parliament. After the Conservative defeat in the 1868 General Election, the party under the leadership of Benjamin Disraeli created the Conservative Central Office to encourage the organisation of constituency associations and to register candidates for elections.

The Emergence of the Labour Party

As the number of voters increased, a third party came into existence with the aim of representing working men in Parliament. As with the Liberal Party 50 to 60 years earlier, the Labour Party was the product both of a new body of voters created by legislation and of the growth of a new ideology.

The earlier parties began as parliamentary groups *within* Parliament and established organisations *outside* it in order to gain support and so achieve re-election. In contrast, the Labour Party began as a movement outside Parliament, seeking representation within it in order to further the aims of party policy. In 1893 an Independent Labour Party was formed in Bradford and, following a meeting in 1900 with some trade unions and socialist societies, a Labour Representation Committee was established to co-ordinate plans for Labour representation in Parliament. After the 1906 Election the Committee became the Labour Party. Local committees were established at constituency level, but there was no individual membership; the Committee consisted entirely of affiliated organisations. In 1918 the Party was completely reorganised, with constituency Labour parties admitting individual members as well as affiliated organisations.

During the inter-war period (1918–39) the Labour Party took the place of the Liberal Party, which had last formed a government by itself in 1906–16, as the main rival of the Conservative Party. The first Labour Government held office for ten months in 1924, although it lacked an overall majority in the House of Commons. In 1929–31 the Party took office for a second time, again as a minority government. Since 1945 there have been eight Conservative and six Labour governments and almost all the members of the House of Commons have represented either the Conservative or the Labour Party. Despite considerable electoral strength in the country (see pp. 50-57), the Liberal Party did not at any time between 1945 and 1988 have more than 19 members in the House of Commons. Its successor is the Liberal Democrats (see below).

The Liberal Democrats

A new political party was formally established in 1981 when a number of MPs and two former Labour ministers, not then in

Parliament, broke away from their parties to form the Social Democratic Party (SDP). At the time of its launch, the parliamentary group of the SDP consisted of 14 MPs—13 former Labour MPs and one former Conservative. The members concerned joined the Council for Social Democracy, set up in 1981 to 'rally all those ... committed to the values, principles and policies of social democracy'. By 1982 the SDP was represented in the House of Commons by 29 MPs.

In the year of its formation the SDP entered into an electoral alliance with the Liberal Party. The two parties entered the 1983 and 1987 General Elections with a joint programme. Their parliamentary candidates offered themselves as Alliance candidates who, if elected, would sit in the House of Commons as members of their respective parties. (The Alliance, unlike the Liberal Party in earlier elections, contested all 633 seats in England, Wales and Scotland.) In the 1987 General Election the Alliance returned 22 members—17 Liberal and five SDP—with over 22 per cent of the total vote.

The Liberal Party and the SDP shared a common approach to major policy issues. Following a ballot of members of both parties, in March 1988 members of the two parties[2] merged to form a new party, the Social & Liberal Democrats. This party is now known as the Liberal Democrats and is represented in the House of Commons by 22 MPs.

Other Parties

Nationalist Parties

Other parties represented in Parliament include the nationalist parties in Scotland and Wales.

[2] After the formation of the Liberal Democrats in 1988, a separate Social Democratic Party continued to exist, comprising those SDP members who opposed the merger; it was represented by three MPs. The SDP voted to suspend the operation of its constitution in June 1990.

The Scottish National Party (SNP) was formed in 1934 by supporters of self-government for Scotland and returned its first MP in a by-election in 1945. It subsequently lost support, but during the 1960s its membership increased and it secured a by-election success in 1967. In 1970 it won its first seat at a General Election. The SNP received its greatest support in the two General Elections in 1974, when the party returned seven MPs in the February election and 11 in October—the only General Elections to date that it has returned more than three MPs.

Like the SNP, Plaid Cymru, the Welsh Nationalist Party (literally 'The Party of Wales'), made considerable advances in membership during the 1960s. Founded in 1925, it secured its first seat in the House of Commons at a by-election in 1966. It contested all 36 Welsh seats for the first time in the 1970 General Election, but failed to return any members to the House of Commons. The party returned two and then three MPs in the two elections of 1974. In the 1992 General Election Plaid Cymru returned four MPs to Westminster.

Northern Ireland

The Conservative and Labour parties and the Liberal Democrats have traditionally operated in England, Wales and Scotland only; they have not been organised in Northern Ireland and have not contested elections there. However, in the early 1990s a number of Conservative constituency associations in Northern Ireland became affiliated to the National Union of Conservative and Unionist Associations (see p. 21), and in the 1992 General Election the Conservative party contested parliamentary seats in Northern Ireland for the first time this century. There are now 11 Conservative constituency associations in Northern Ireland.

All the main political parties in Northern Ireland are locally based, and elected representatives from Northern Ireland constituencies at Westminster (the numbers of which increased from 12 to 17 in 1979) are drawn from four political parties. The largest is the Ulster Unionist party, with nine members.

The Party System

The Electoral System

In the British electoral system the country is divided into 651 single-member constituencies. Representatives are elected to Parliament by the first-past-the-post (simple majority) method, which awards seats in the House of Commons to the candidates with the largest number of votes in each constituency. The boundaries of the constituencies are reviewed every 10 to 15 years to take account of population movements or other changes. Under this system the strongest party in the House of Commons may have an absolute majority of seats with less than an absolute majority of votes. The system is generally considered to favour two-party competition, especially between parties whose support is concentrated geographically, and to discriminate against parties with support spread across constituencies.

In the 1992 General Election, for example, support for the Conservative Party was greatest in the south-east of England, with the exception of inner London, while that for the Labour Party was greatest in the north of England and in Wales; support for the Liberal Democrats, on the other hand, was fairly evenly distributed throughout Great Britain. (A percentage distribution of the votes cast in each region for the main parties in the 1992 Election appears in Table 1).

Table 1: Percentage Distribution of Votes Cast in Each Region by Main Party

	Conservative	Labour	Lib Dem
England	45.5	33.9	19.2
North	33.4	50.6	15.6
Yorkshire and Humberside	37.9	44.3	16.8
East Midlands	46.6	37.4	15.3
East Anglia	51.0	28.0	19.5
Greater London	45.3	37.1	15.1
Rest of South East	54.5	20.8	23.3
South West	47.6	19.2	31.4
West Midlands	44.8	38.8	15.0
North West	37.8	44.9	15.8
Wales	28.6	49.5	12.4
Scotland	25.6	39.0	13.1
N. Ireland	5.7	–	–

Sources: *The British General Election of 1992*, by D. Butler and D. Kavanagh and *Times Guide to the House of Commons April 1992* (see Further Reading, pp. 61–2).

Forming a Government

The party which wins most seats (though not necessarily the most votes) at a General Election, or which has the support of a majority of members in the House of Commons, is usually invited by the Sovereign to form a government. The party with the next largest number of seats is officially recognised as 'Her Majesty's Opposition'; this has its own leader, who is paid a salary from public funds, and its own 'shadow cabinet'. Members of other parties, or any independent MPs who have been elected, support or oppose the government according to their party or their own view of the policy being debated at any given time. Because the official Opposition is a minority party, it seldom succeeds in introducing or amending legislation. However, its statements and policies are important, since it is considered to be a potential government—and would become so if successful at the next General Election.

On occasion, a minority government may be formed or arise. In some cases no one party succeeds in winning a majority of seats over all the other parties combined (as after the General Election of February 1974). Following the defeat and resignation of the Government, it is customary in such circumstances for the Sovereign to invite the leader of the largest opposition party in the House of Commons to form a government. A minority government may also arise when, during the life of a Parliament, the governing party loses its majority through by-election defeats, as the Labour Government did in 1977. In both these circumstances, the Government has three choices:

—it may introduce only that legislation which commands the support of a majority in the House;

—it may make some form of arrangement with one or more opposition parties to enable it to stay in office; or

—it can ask for Parliament to be dissolved and for a General Election to be held.

A minority government may stay in office so long as all other parties do not form a united parliamentary opposition to its policies and defeat it on a vote of confidence. Occasionally a minority administration has made a formal agreement with another party to support it. This occurred in March 1977 when the Labour Government made a formal agreement with the parliamentary

Liberal Party whereby Liberal MPs agreed to 'work with the Government in the pursuit of economic recovery'. The 'Lib–Lab Pact', as it was called, lasted until the autumn of 1978, when Liberal support was withdrawn.

The formation of a coalition government in Britain has taken place during this century only for the sake of overcoming national crises, such as the two world wars (1914–18 and 1939–45) or the economic depression during the 1930s. In a coalition, ministers are drawn from each of the parties concerned. The last coalition in Britain was dissolved in 1945 towards the end of the Second World War.

The party system assumes that, in spite of the alternative programmes sponsored by the main political parties, there is common interest and agreement upon the maintenance of free institutions and parliamentary democracy.

The General Election of April 1992

The last General Election was held on 9 April 1992, when the Conservative Party gained a majority of 21 seats over all other parties. The total number of electors entitled to vote in the Election was some 43.3 million, and 76.9 per cent of the electorate voted. Table 2 shows the number of seats and votes obtained by each party at present represented in Parliament and their percentage share of the total vote. For the current state of the parties in the House of Commons, see p. 58.

Errata Slip

Please substitute this table for the existing Table 2 on page 13, which contains errors.

Table 2: General Election Result 1992 (9 April)

Party	Total votes	MPs elected	Candi- dates	% Share of votes
Conservative[a]	14,093,007	336	645	41.9
Labour	11,560,094	271	634	34.4
Liberal Democrats	5,999,606	20	632	17.8
Plaid Cymru[b]	156,796	4	38	0.5
Scottish National	629,564	3	72	1.9
Ulster Unionist	271,049	9	13	0.8
Democratic Unionist	103,039	3	7	0.3
Social Democratic and Labour	184,445	4	13	0.5
Ulster Popular Unionist	19,305	1	1	0.1
Sinn Fein	78,291	—	14	0.2
Alliance	68,665	—	16	0.2
Green	170,047	—	253	0.5
Liberal	64,744	—	73	0.2
Natural Law	62,888	—	309	0.2
Others	152,534	—	229	0.5

[a] Includes 11 candidates in Northern Ireland, four of whom lost their deposits.
[b] Plaid Cymru totals include three joint Plaid Cymru/Green candidates.

Table 2: General Election Result 1992 (9 April)

Party	Total votes	MPs elected	Candi- dates	% Share of votes
Conservative[a]	14,093,007	336	645	41.9
Labour	11,560,094	271	634	34.4
Liberal Democrats	5,999,606	20	632	17.8
Scottish National	629,564	3	72	1.9
Plaid Cymru[b]	156,796	4	38	0.5
Northern Ireland parties	785,093	17	100	2.1
Northern Ireland Parties:				
Ulster Unionist	271,049	9	13	0.8
Social Democratic and Labour	184,445	4	13	0.5
Democratic Unionist	103,039	3	7	0.3
Ulster Popular Unionist	19,305	1	1	0.1
Sinn Fein	78,291	—	14	10.0
Alliance	68,665	—	16	8.7
Conservative	44,608	—	11	5.7
Others	15,691	—	25	2.1

[a] Includes 11 candidates in Northern Ireland, four of whom lost their deposits.
[b] Plaid Cymru totals include three joint Plaid Cymru/Green candidates.

Party Organisation Outside Parliament

Although there are important differences, certain elements are common to the organisation outside Parliament of each of the three main parties. Outside Parliament, the basic unit of organisation is the local constituency association. (However, local parties of the Liberal Democrats may cover one or more neighbouring constituencies—see p. 17.) These are usually linked together in regional federations. Also common to each party is a national organisation whose main function is to arrange an annual conference, which provides a channel of communication between the leading members of the party in Parliament and its supporters in the country. A further common feature is a central office, the national headquarters of the party, staffed by professional workers and providing a link between the party in Parliament and the party in the country. Finally, there is the leader of the party. The roles of the party organisation and the importance of the annual party conference, however, vary between parties.

Constituency Associations or Parties

Conservative Party
Conservative constituency associations are composed of individual members who live in, or are connected with, the constituency or have business interests there, and pay a subscription each year to party funds. In many associations there are separate sections catering

for the special interests of women; in most, there is a section for 'Young Conservatives' between the ages of 15 and 30. The Young Conservatives is the largest voluntary political youth movement in Britain.

The associations have complete autonomy in the day-to-day management of their affairs. They are free to elect their own officers, select and appoint their own agents, raise their own funds, and plan and carry out their own publicity programmes. They also conduct election campaigns in their constituencies in their own way, and adopt their own candidates for parliamentary and local government elections (the former normally from a list of names approved by the Party's standing advisory committee on candidates).

There is a fairly wide variety in the structure of associations throughout the country, but in most of them the principal officers are the president, the chairman, three vice-chairmen (those of the constituency political, women's and Young Conservatives' committees) and the honorary treasurer. The governing body is normally the executive council, which is presided over by the chairman of the association and served by the agent in the capacity of secretary. The council deals with all matters affecting the association and elects representatives to the national and area organisations. It also appoints, annually, a number of committees, including a finance and general purposes committee and those dealing with such subjects as political education, trade union affairs and local government.

In constituencies where the Conservative Party is highly organised, branches of the constituency association are set up in each ward or polling district for conducting normal constituency work. A number of local branch members are usually named as representatives from the branch to the executive council of the constituency association to act as a channel of communication between the branch and the association as a whole.

The individual membership of the Party is over half a million.

Labour Party

Labour constituency associations are known as Constituency Labour Parties. Within these parties branches may be formed, usually covering electoral wards in towns, and parishes or groups of parishes in rural areas. The Party has two classes of membership: affiliated organisations and individual members. Affiliated organisations include trade unions (the most important category); co-operative societies and branches of the Co-operative Party (the political wing of the Co-operative Movement—see p. 48); and branches of socialist societies or professional organisations which are affiliated to the Labour Party nationally. Individual members must be aged 15 or over and must be attached to the appropriate branch operating in the area where they live or, for those of voting age, where they are registered as parliamentary or local government electors. Members must accept and conform to the principles and policy of the Labour Party, and they must, if applicable, belong to a trade union affiliated to the Trades Union Congress (TUC) or to a union recognised by the General Council of the TUC as a trade union. Women's sections and branches of Young Labour provide additional facilities for women members and for young members aged up to 27 years.

The constituency parties run their own affairs, elect their own officers, raise and administer their own funds and undertake their own publicity programmes. They select their candidates and appoint their agents subject to the approval of the national organisation, and conduct election campaigns in the constituency on behalf of the Party.

The affairs of the constituency parties are controlled by a general committee, which consists of delegates elected by the affiliated organisations, branches of individual members and women's and youth sections; all must be individual members of the Party.

An executive committee is elected annually by the general committee from among its own members to direct the work of the association under its supervision. The executive committee normally consists of the officers of the constituency party (the president or chair, two vice-chairs, treasurer and secretary, constituency women's officer and constituency youth/student officer) and as many additional members as the general committee thinks appropriate. The executive committee may set up sub-committees to deal with the social and recreational aspects of the work of the constituency party, with the distribution of publicity material, and with the usual range of political activity. The estimated individual membership of the Party is around 270,000. There are an additional 4.5 million affiliated members who subscribe through their trade union organisations.

Liberal Democrats

The basic unit of organisation is the local party, usually covering a single parliamentary constituency, although some may cover more than one constituency in the same region, county, metropolitan district or London borough, subject to the agreement of the members. The minimum number of members is 30. The local party is a successor to the former Liberal Party and Social Democratic Party organisations in its area. Local parties are responsible for their own organisation, working arrangements and finance; they sponsor Liberal Democrat candidates in local and national elections. They are also expected to keep watch on the legislative and administrative work of the Government, especially as it affects the needs and interests of the district and the local council. They are responsible for directing the attention of local authorities, the public and the press to the importance of these subjects, and to the methods by which Liberal Democrats believe they should be handled.

There are very approximately 101,000 individual party members.

Constituency Agents

In each constituency, an agent is appointed by each party as the chief organiser of party activities in the area. Some of these agents are full-time salaried officials, who hold certificates (issued by the party headquarters) guaranteeing their knowledge of election law and allied matters. There are also many part-time or voluntary agents, particularly in the Labour and Liberal Democrat parties. The duties of the agent may include acting as secretary to the constituency association and serving as executive assistant to the local MP. Before elections, the agent is also expected to act as business manager to the prospective candidate and to ensure that election campaigns are conducted within the law. In constituencies where there is no full-time agent, part-time or voluntary election agents or organisers, particularly in the case of the Liberal Democrats, may be appointed. The salaries of most agents are met from constituency association funds, but the Labour Party head office contributes towards the cost of 28 agents in key constituencies, and also employs a number of organisers who cover more than one constituency.

Parliamentary Candidates

Prospective candidates are chosen by the constituency associations of each party according to its own established practice. Sitting MPs in all parties have to be readopted by their constituency associations at some point before contesting a General Election.

Procedure in the *Conservative Party* is as follows: when a new candidate is to be chosen, the executive council of the constituency association appoints a selection committee to which the standing advisory committee on candidates at party headquarters submits a list of potential candidates who have indicated their wish to stand for that constituency. The names of local party members, some of whom may have put forward their own names for consideration, are also submitted. When any new local names have been approved by the standing committee, the selection committee chooses a number of candidates for interview, and produces a shortlist to appear before the whole executive council. A series of ballots is then taken, as a result of which one candidate may be recommended to a general meeting of the whole constituency association. Except on the rarest occasions, this candidate is formally adopted. In recent years an increasing number of constituency associations have presented a choice of two or three potential candidates, chosen by the executive council, to a general meeting, rather than just one recommended candidate.

In the *Labour Party*, when a decision has been made (in consultation with the national organisation) to contest an election and a new candidate is to be chosen, party and affiliated organisations within the constituency are invited to nominate a candidate. A nomination may also be made by the executive committee of the constituency association but individuals may not submit their own names. The general committee of the Constituency Labour Party then examines all nominations and proposes a shortlist. This list is submitted to individual party members on a one member one vote basis using the system of single transferable vote. The nominee receiving over 50 per cent at the final stage of the count becomes the candidate.

The Labour Party requires parliamentary candidates, including MPs, to be reselected by the local party between elections. In the case of a sitting MP, party branches and affiliated organisations are invited to make nominations. If two thirds of these bodies nominate the sitting MP, he or she is automatically reselected. If, on the other hand, this proportion falls below two thirds, the normal candidate selection procedure follows on the basis of individual one member one vote. His or her name is then placed before a meeting of the NEC for endorsement.

The *Liberal Democrats*' procedure involves the shortlisting of candidates by the executive committee of the local party or a shortlisting sub-committee appointed by it. All candidates must be included in the Party's list of approved candidates. Except in cases where the sitting MP or previous candidate is to be reselected, a specified minimum number of candidates must be shortlisted. Shortlists of two to four candidates must include at least one member of each sex (subject to there being a sufficient number of applicants of each sex), with due regard also being paid to the representation of ethnic minorities. All members of the local party are entitled to participate in voting to select a candidate; the system used is the alternative vote method. The sitting MP may be reselected at a general meeting of the local party.

Regional Organisation

The constituency associations of the Conservative, Labour and Liberal Democrat Parties are grouped into regional organisations which bring together party political opinion over a wide region and so are able to provide co-ordinated advice and information for the central organisation and party leaders.

The Conservative Party has 11 'provincial' areas in England and Wales, each having an area council on which all the constituencies in the area are represented. Scotland is split into five areas, each with an area council to which eight representatives are sent by each constituency in the region.

The Labour Party has nine regional councils, whose membership is open to the following bodies: constituency parties affiliated to the Labour Party at national level; county (regional in Scotland) Labour parties; trade unions affiliated to the Labour Party and the TUC at national level; district councils of nationally affiliated trade unions; co-operative societies or organisations; socialist societies affiliated to the Labour Party nationally; and women's councils. There are also district Labour parties which correspond to the areas of local government district councils.

The Liberal Democrats are organised as a federal party, with autonomous state parties in England, Scotland and Wales, all with their own national offices, staff and conferences. The state party in England is further subdivided into 12 regional parties. The federal party, which holds its own conferences, shares its headquarters with the English state party and carries out many organisational tasks, such as membership administration and policy development.

National Organisation

Conservative Party
The central pillar of the party organisation in England and Wales is the National Union of Conservative and Unionist[3] Associations, a federal organisation to which are affiliated around 600 constituency

---

[3] The word 'Unionist' in the title stems from the amalgamation in 1912 of the Conservative Party and the Liberal Unionists who had broken away from the rest of the Liberal Party in 1886 over a dispute concerning Home Rule for Ireland, in which they favoured continued union with that country.

associations. Scotland has its own organisation, the Scottish Conservative and Unionist Association, but its 72 constituency associations are now also affiliated to the National Union. The main functions of the National Union are to advance the Party's cause, to give an opportunity for issues to be debated, and to serve as an advisory body which keeps the leader informed of party opinion. In 1993 a Board of Management was established to give wide-ranging guidance to the campaigning, communications and organisational work of the Conservative Party at all levels by bringing together the elected, voluntary and professional parts of the Party.

The governing body of the National Union is the Central Council, which meets once a year in the spring to debate motions which have been submitted from constituencies, areas, and national advisory committees. It also elects the officers of the National Union. Membership includes the leader of the Party and other principal officers and officials; the Conservative members of both Houses of Parliament and of the European Parliament; the members of the Executive Committee; and six representatives from each constituency association, together with representatives from the Scottish Association, provincial area councils, and national committees.

The Executive Committee of the National Union (which meets regularly) is composed of 264 members, including representatives of the provincial area councils (who, in turn, represent the constituencies in the areas) and other provincial officers of the Party. The Committee has authority to act on behalf of the Central Council in the intervals between the latter's meetings. Its functions include: recommending to the Central Council candidates for election as officers of the National Union; approving the admission of constituency associations to the National Union; settling disputes between or within constituency associations; considering proposals on party or public affairs from the provincial areas or constituencies and forwarding them to the appropriate quarters. It also elects representatives of the National Union to the various national committees of the Party and submits an annual report to the party conference. The Executive Committee is advised by the following National Advisory Committees: Women, Young Conservatives, Trade Unionists, Local Government, Education, and the Conservative Political Centre National Advisory Committee.

There are also a number of other central committees or boards, some of which report to the Executive Committee, and they occupy an important place in party organisation. They are: the Conservative Party Board of Finance; the Standing Advisory Committees on United Kingdom and European Candidates; the Examination Board (for agents and organisers); and the Superannuation Fund.

An annual conference, lasting four days, is held by the National Union every year and is the most important annual gathering of the Party. The conference is attended by the members of the Central Council and two additional representatives of each constituency— one of whom must be a Young Conservative—including certificated agents or organisers. At the conference the National Union receives the report of the Executive Committee, and debates and passes resolutions on party policy. It is not authorised to decide on policy and has no executive power; its resolutions are therefore not binding on the party leadership, but they have considerable influence. Annual conferences are also held by the Party in Scotland and Wales.

Labour Party

The highest authority in the Labour Party is the party conference, which controls the work of the Party outside Parliament, is responsible for its constitution and standing orders, and decides, in broad outline, party policy. The conference is normally held once a year for four and a half days and is attended by some 1,300 delegates appointed by trade unions, constituency parties and socialist and co-operative societies. Ex officio members, such as leading officials of the Party, MPs and prospective parliamentary candidates, and constituency party agents, take part.

Seventy per cent of the votes at the conference are held by the trade unions, distributed in proportion to the money that each union pays annually as an affiliation fee; the payment is made from union members' contributions to political funds.

The NEC is the administrative authority of the Party and seeks to apply its policies between annual party conferences. It consists of 29 members, three of whom are ex officio—the leader, the deputy leader of the Party, and one youth member elected at the National Youth Conference. The treasurer and 25 members are elected every year at the annual conference, on the following basis: 12 members by the trade union delegates; seven by a one member one vote postal ballot; one by the delegates of socialist, co-operative and professional organisations; and five women members elected by the conference as a whole (as is the treasurer). The NEC elects its own chair and vice-chair every year. Its functions are to supervise the work of the Party outside Parliament at every level, and to report on its own work to the conference. It submits to conference 'such resolutions and declarations affecting the programme, principles and policy of the Party as, in its view, may be necessitated by political circumstances'.

The NEC works through a number of committees (Organisation, International, Development and Policy, Elections and Campaigns, Women, Youth, Finance and General Purposes, and Disputes). Two of these (the International and Policy committees) have a number of special sub-committees and working parties appointed to deal with particular areas of policy or problems of current concern to the Party. The leader of the Party, the deputy leader, and the chair, vice-chair and the treasurer of the NEC are ex officio members of each committee; the remaining members are elected through the NEC itself.

The NEC also participates in a number of general committees with other representative Labour organisations. The Fabian Society[4] is affiliated to the Labour Party; it publishes pamphlets on social, economic, political and international issues, many of which aim to influence Labour Party policy.

Liberal Democrats

The Liberal Democrats determine party policy through the Federal Conference. This is attended by representatives of local parties, associated organisations representing youth and students, the Party's parliamentary team and the party officers. The Conference normally meets twice a year, in spring and autumn. It receives reports from the Party's Federal Executive, the Federal Policy Committee and the Federal Conference Committee.

The Federal Policy Committee is responsible for developing and presenting party policy, including the preparation of the general election manifesto. The Committee consists of the party leader, the president, five representatives of the Party in both Houses of Parliament, three principal local authority councillors, two representatives of each of the Scottish and Welsh parties, and 15 members elected by the Federal Conference.

The Federal Executive, whose membership is elected on a similar basis to the Federal Policy Committee, is responsible for directing, co-ordinating and implementing the work of the federal party. Its responsibilities include establishing a Finance and Administration Committee, which manages the finances and directs the administration of the federal party, including its head-quarters, and a campaigns and communications committee, responsible for co-ordinating the campaigning work of the party.

In England, Scotland and Wales the Liberal Democrats constitute separate state parties. Regional parties in England may also

[4] A socialist intellectual group founded in 1884 with some local branches.

seek recognition as state parties but so far none have sought to. The state parties have separate organisations and hold their own conferences; together they form the federal party.

Central Offices
Each main party has a national headquarters, staffed by full-time professional workers who co-ordinate the party organisation and prepare various party publications, including general outlines of policy and pamphlets on particular topics.

The *Conservative* Central Office, along with its recently formed seven regional offices, is presided over by a chairman, assisted by two deputy chairmen and four vice-chairmen of the party organisation and six treasurers. The chairman, who is appointed by the leader of the Party, is in charge of Central Office and has overall responsibility for maintaining the nationwide organisation of the Party. The two deputy chairmen and four vice-chairmen are responsible respectively for communications and youth, parliamentary candidates, international affairs, local government, women, and campaigning. All these appointments are made by the leader of the Party. There is a separate Central Office in Scotland with its own chairman.

Central Office has five principal divisions: Party Campaigning, Communications, Constituency Services, Administration and Finance, and the Research Department. Smaller departments within these divisions include constituency computer services, speakers, training, trade unions, local government, women and youth. In 1993 a new post of Director-General was established at Conservative Central Office, with responsibility for day-to-day management.

The Conservative Research Department, which is responsible to the party leader through the party chairman, plays an important part in developing party policies. On a day-to-day basis, the Research Department is responsible for briefing the parliamentary party (including the Cabinet when the Conservative Party is in power) and servicing Conservative backbench committees. It provides factual material for party publicity and produces reference works. It has three major sections: economic, home affairs, and political. Working alongside it are the International Office and the Conservative Political Centre. The International Office provides briefing on aspects of foreign policy, maintains contact with parties of the right worldwide, assists liaison between the European Parliament and Westminster, and acts as the point of first contact with the Party for organisations and individuals from other countries, foreign journalists and diplomatic missions. The Conservative Political Centre provides political education facilities for party members and others interested in politics, through constituency discussion groups, seminars, weekend schools, and publications by MPs and others.

The headquarters of the *Labour Party* is composed of the General Secretary's Office and four directorates dealing with development and organisation, policy development, campaigns and elections, and the media. The chief official is the General Secretary, who works under the direction of the NEC, and is appointed by the annual conference on the recommendation of the NEC.

The General Secretary, as chief executive, is concerned with the entire work of the Party. The International Secretary is responsible for maintaining contacts with socialist parties in foreign countries and in the Commonwealth.[5] All the directorates are responsible to committees of the NEC; the General Secretary reports directly to the NEC itself.

[5] The Labour Party is a member of the Socialist International, which consists of over 90 labour, democratic socialist parties in various countries throughout the world.

The headquarters of the *Liberal Democrats* is responsible to the Finance and Administration Committee, which consists of the treasurer, the president, one representative of each state party, the Federal Chief Executive, two elected representatives of staff employed by the federal party, and five members elected by the Federal Executive. The Federal Executive appoints a salaried General Secretary, who is responsible for the employment of the staff of the federal party. Federal party staff are organised into six departments: General Secretary's; membership and direct mail; finance; campaigns and elections (including the party newspapers); policy; and conference. The offices of the Youth and Student Liberal Democrats and the Women Liberal Democrats are also situated at party headquarters. The Councillors' Association, which is an important body in the party's campaigning and local government activities, has separate staff and headquarters.

Party Finance

The main parties receive their funds from various sources. The central income of the Conservative Party comes from voluntary subscriptions consisting of individual as well as company contributions. Additional contributions from the constituency associations are assessed on an agreed basis. There is no fixed subscription.

Just over 50 per cent of the income of the Labour Party is provided by annual affiliation fees for each member paid by trade unions, socialist societies and one large co-operative society. The remainder is provided by the constituency associations on the basis of individual membership, each individual member paying a minimum annual subscription of £15, with reduced rates of £5 for students, the elderly and the unemployed.

The Liberal Democrats' funds consist of subscriptions and donations from individual members of the local parties. The minimum annual subscription is £3; the recommended annual sub-scription £22. The Federal Conference determines the proportion of the state parties' subscriptions which it receives. Each state party's conference similarly determines the division between its own and the local parties' funds.

In 1993 the Conservative Party received a central income of just over £11.5 million; in 1992 the Labour Party's central income was £8.5 million; and the central income of the Liberal Democrat headquarters in London was about £1.5 million.

No political party is legally obliged to publish its accounts. However, business firms required to publish their accounts under the Companies Act 1967 must show the amounts of contributions above £200 made to political party funds.

The Party Leaders

The power of the party leaders and the method of their appoint-ment differ among the parties. However in all cases when a party wins a General Election, it is the leader who is called upon by the Sovereign to form a government. As Prime Minister he or she is then entitled to choose the members of the administration.

In the Conservative Party, the party leader is elected by Conservative MPs in a secret ballot. In the Labour Party, the lead-er's appointment is decided on a broader basis—through election at party conference by representatives of the affiliated trade unions, individual members, and the parliamentary party. The Liberal Democrats' party leader, and its president, are elected by a postal vote by party members.

Once elected, the leaders of the Conservative, Labour and Liberal Democrat Parties become the national leaders of their parties inside and outside Parliament.

The leader of the Conservative Party is the Prime Minister, John Major, MP, (elected as leader in 1990); the late John Smith, MP, was leader of the Labour Party from 1992 to May 1994. Paddy Ashdown, MP, became the first elected leader of the Liberal Democrats in 1988.

Conservative Party

The leader is subject to annual re-election within 28 days of the opening of a new parliamentary session, or within six months of a General Election. The Conservative leader is elected by Conservative MPs, who nominate candidates.

If necessary, there are three ballots. A candidate is elected on the first ballot if he or she receives both an overall majority of votes and 15 per cent more of the total vote than any other candidate. Conservative constituency associations, Conservative peers and Conservative members of the European Parliament are given an opportunity to make their views known. If no winner emerges on the first ballot, a second one is held and nominations for the first are void. Candidates who did not stand in the first ballot may stand in the second. The winner of the second ballot is the candidate receiving more than 50 per cent of votes. If there is no second ballot winner, a third ballot may be organised. The three candidates receiving the highest number of votes at the second ballot go forward to the final ballot, where voters indicate their first and second choices. The candidate with the lowest number of first preferences is eliminated and the votes of those giving him or her as their first preference are redistributed among the other two in accordance with their second preferences.

Once the result of the election has been declared, the winner is presented for confirmation as leader of the Conservative Party to a

A nineteenth-century political cartoon. The two main parties at the time were the Liberals and the Conservatives (see p. 3).

General Election 1992: John Major, returning to 10 Downing Street as Prime Minister, answers questions from reporters.

COI Pictures

A strategy meeting of Labour's shadow cabinet, February 1993: the late John Smith, then leader of the Party, with deputy leader Margaret Beckett and shadow chancellor Gordon Brown.

PA/Fiona Hanson

A Liberal
Democrat Party
Conference
(see p. 28).

Alex Salmond canvassing
for the Scottish National
Party in April 1992

Plaid Cymru's newly founded
policy cabinet after its first
meeting in Cardiff, February 1994
(see p. 39).

Children of West Belfast keeping Dr Joe Hendron (Socialist Democratic and Labour) company as he canvasses in the constituency (April 1992). He was later elected as MP.

An Ulster Unionist Party poster.

meeting of Conservative MPs and peers, adopted parliamentary candidates and members of the Executive Committee of the National Union of Conservative and Unionist Associations.

The Conservative Party leader is responsible for the formulation of party policy. Although kept constantly aware through the various party organisations of the feelings and opinions of Conservative supporters throughout the country, the party leader is not normally required to report on his or her work either inside or outside Parliament. The Conservative leader normally attends most sessions of the Party's annual conference and addresses the representatives.

When the Party is in opposition the Conservative leader chooses a 'shadow cabinet' of about 18 MPs and peers to serve as a consultative committee. The leader is also in charge of the party headquarters with the right to appoint all its officers. The powers of the Conservative leader are exercised only with the consent of the Party; if there is clear evidence that this consent is being withdrawn, the leader has no alternative but to resign.

Labour Party

The leader of the Labour Party, like that of the Conservative Party, is subject to annual re-election when in opposition. When the Party is in office, elections for the leadership take place only when a vacancy occurs through the death or resignation of the Prime Minister.

Candidates for election to the Labour Party leadership must be MPs and must be nominated by 12.5 per cent of the parliamentary party when a vacancy occurs, and 20 per cent when there is no vacancy. They are elected by an electoral college consisting of representatives from the affiliated trade unions, the constituency parties and the House of Commons members of the parliamentary party in equal ratios. The successful candidate is the one who receives an overall majority of the votes cast, and successive ballots are held until this occurs. If after the first ballot no candidate has an overall majority, the candidate with the lowest vote drops out (or the two or three lowest-placed candidates if their combined votes amount to fewer than those of the candidates above them). After the first ballot, other candidates may withdraw if they wish, but no new candidate may be nominated. The deputy leader of the Party is elected annually in the same way.

The function of the Labour Party leader is to implement, as far as possible, the programme determined jointly by the Parliamentary Labour Party and the party organisations. He or she attends the annual party conference to report on the work done in Parliament during the previous year. When leader of the Opposition, the party leader works with a 'shadow cabinet' (the Parliamentary Committee, see p. 37) whose members are chosen by the Parliamentary Labour Party. The leader appoints the official spokesmen from the members of the elected Parliamentary Committee and other members of the Parliamentary Labour Party. The leader and his or her deputy are ex officio members of the NEC, which directs the operations of the party headquarters, but he or she is not in personal control.

Liberal Democrats

Unless postponed by a vote of two-thirds of the Federal Executive, elections for the leader of the Party have to be held once every Parliament. Otherwise an election is held either at the leader's own request or in the following circumstances: if the leader loses his or her seat in Parliament; if a majority of Liberal Democrat MPs pass a vote of no confidence in the leader; or at the request of 75 local parties following the holding of general meetings at which a quorum of members is present.

Candidates for the Liberal Democrat leadership must be members of the party in the House of Commons, proposed and seconded by Liberal Democrat MPs, and supported by 200 party members in 20 local parties or youth or student associated organisations.

Elections for the post of president of the party are held every two years. The president chairs the Federal Executive.

Party Organisation Inside Parliament

The Whips

In Parliament the parties are managed by officers known as 'Whips', who are MPs and peers (chosen within their parliamentary party). Their duties include informing members of forthcoming parliamentary business; maintaining the party's voting strength by ensuring that members attend important debates and support their party in divisions (the taking of votes); and passing on to the party leadership the opinions of backbench members.

In the House of Commons the party whips consist of the Chief Whip and, in the two main parties, the Deputy Chief Whip and a varying number of junior whips, all of whom are MPs. Those of the party in power are known as Government Whips and are paid out of public funds.

There are Government and Opposition Whips in both Houses of Parliament, but the whips in the House of Lords are less exclusively concerned with party matters and, unlike those in the Commons, may act as government spokesmen and spokeswomen.

The Government Chief Whip is directly answerable to the Prime Minister and the Leader of the House of Commons. Subject to the Cabinet, the overriding responsibility for the progress of the Government's legislative programmes rests with the Leader of the House. Under the authority of the Leader, the Government Chief Whip in the Commons attends the Cabinet and makes the day-to-day arrangements for the Government's programme of business (estimating the time likely to be required for each item and discussing the proposed business arrangements with the Opposition). The Chief Whip is also responsible for securing majorities for the Government. He or she is assisted by a very small Civil Service staff, headed by the Private Secretary, who is frequently consulted by the Leader of the House. The Opposition Chief Whip carries out similar duties for his or her own party, and also receives a special salary. Two other Opposition Whips in the House of Commons also receive official salaries.

The Government and Opposition Chief Whips meet frequently. Together they constitute the 'usual channels' often referred to in the House of Commons when the question of finding time for debating an issue or other parliamentary arrangements is discussed.

The Opposition Chief Whip receives advance notice of the Government's programme each week, and no final decision is taken until after he or she has met the Government Chief Whip. The junior whips are responsible for keeping in touch with individual MPs and passing on their opinions to the Chief Whip. There are about 12 whips on each side, each responsible for 20 to 30 MPs, usually grouped on a regional basis.

In the House of Lords both the Government Chief Whip and the Opposition Chief Whip receive a salary from public funds. The Government Chief Whip is assisted by Government Whips who, as in the House of Commons, are paid; the Opposition Whips are not paid an official salary.

Party Organisation

The most important organ of the Conservative Party in Parliament is the Conservative and Unionist Members' Committee, popularly known as the 1922 Committee. This Committee, named after the year in which it was formed, normally meets once a week and consists of the backbench membership of the Conservative Party in the House of Commons. It is not authorised to decide policy or to control directly the activities of the Party's leader or front bench.

However, it serves to represent Conservative opinion in the House of Commons, and it is upon this Committee's support that the leader's position in the Party depends. The Committee is autonomous and independent; it has its own organisation and its own members. When the Conservative Party is in office, ministers attend its meetings by invitation and not by right; but when the Conservatives are in opposition, all members of the Party in the Commons may attend meetings. The Committee is presided over by a chairman (elected annually), two vice-chairmen, two secretaries and a treasurer. Together with 12 others elected by the Committee from among its members these constitute an executive committee. This meets weekly, immediately before the meeting of the full Committee. Major issues of party or government policy are discussed at meetings of the 1922 Committee, but votes are not normally taken. Instead the chairman is expected to interpret 'the sense of the meeting'.

There are no members of the House of Lords in the 1922 Committee: Conservative peers hold their meetings separately as members of the Association of Conservative Peers. When the Party is in opposition, the leader appoints the consultative committee which acts as the Party's 'shadow cabinet' and is separate from the executive committee of the 1922 Committee.

The Parliamentary Labour Party (PLP) is composed of all Labour members in both Houses of Parliament. When the Labour Party is in office, a parliamentary committee acts as a channel of communication between the Government and its backbenchers in both Houses. Half of the committee is elected by the backbench Labour members of the House of Commons and the remainder are representatives of the Government. These include the Leader of the House, the Government Chief Whip and four others, including a Labour peer, appointed by the party leader. When Labour is in opposition, the PLP is run by an elected parliamentary committee (the 'shadow cabinet') consisting of six ex officio members. These are the leader of the party, the deputy leader, the chair of the parliamentary party, the Labour Chief Whips from both Houses of Parliament, and the leader of the Labour peers. Its other members are 18 elected representatives of Labour MPs and one elected representative of the Labour peers. For ballot papers to be valid in this election three votes must be cast for women candidates if three or more are nominated.

Meetings of the PLP, at which broad outlines of policy are discussed and important decisions sometimes taken, are held at least twice a week, and may be convened more often. The party leader and his or her colleagues are expected to attend and do so whenever possible, whether the Party is in or out of office. In general, the PLP has a greater measure of influence over policy than its Conservative counterpart.

The Liberal Democrats meet each week to discuss forthcoming parliamentary business and other matters; the leader takes the chair. All MPs and several peers attend.

Party Committees

As well as attending party meetings, both Conservative and Labour MPs have a policy committee system, organised around subject areas roughly corresponding to those of government departments. Both main parties have about 20 groups of this kind, including, for instance, agriculture and food, defence, finance, trade and industry, education, health and foreign and Commonwealth affairs.

In the Parliamentary Labour Party there are also regional groups. The Liberal Democrats' Federal Policy Committee establishes policy working groups to prepare policy papers to be debated by conference, and to provide policy advice to MPs and peers; the relevant parliamentary spokesmen are automatically members.

Financial Assistance to Opposition Parties

Annual financial assistance is given from public funds to help opposition parties carry out their parliamentary work at Westminster. Assistance is limited to parties which had at least two members elected at the previous General Election, or one member elected and a minimum of 150,000 votes cast. The amounts payable have been revised on six occasions since the inception of the scheme in 1975. In November 1993 the House of Commons agreed to increase these payments each year by reference to the retail prices index. From April 1994 the amount given is £3,442.50 for every seat won and £6.89 for every 200 votes.

In November 1993 the House also agreed to establish a fund of £100,000 for Opposition travel in connection with front-bench duties. This is to be distributed and uprated on the same basis as the main financial assistance.

The total amounts payable in 1994–95 to each opposition party are: Labour Party £1,454,613; Liberal Democrats £301,087; Scottish National Party £34,979; Plaid Cymru (Welsh Nationalist) £20,942; Ulster Unionist Party £44,057; Democratic Unionist Party £15,163; and Social Democratic and Labour Party £21,989. Parties are accountable for expenditure to the Accounting Officer of the House of Commons. The allocation of a party's entitlement between its work in the House of Commons and the House of Lords is decided by the party itself.

The Nationalist Parties: Plaid Cymru and the Scottish National Party

Plaid Cymru (Welsh Nationalist) returned four members to Parliament, and the Scottish National Party (SNP) three, in the 1992 General Election. Plaid Cymru received 156,796 votes or 9 per cent of the total vote in Wales; the SNP received 629,564 votes or 21.5 per cent of the total vote in Scotland.

The organisation of the two parties, which has many features in common, is outlined below.

Branches and Constituency Associations

The basic unit of organisation in both Plaid Cymru and the Scottish National Party is the branch, rather than the constituency association. This is partly due to the large geographical area of many constituencies in the rural regions of Scotland and Wales, which makes it convenient to organise parties at a more local level. Delegates from the branches of both parties are appointed to the constituency associations. Both Plaid Cymru and the SNP consist of individual members who pay an annual membership fee; the SNP also has three affiliated organisations. In both parties parliamentary candidates are chosen by the constituency associations in consultation with their respective National Executive Committees.

National Organisation

The annual conference of Plaid Cymru is the supreme authority within the Party. Between conferences, which are attended by delegates from the branches, the National Council assumes responsibility for taking policy decisions. It comprises two representatives from each constituency, together with prospective parliamentary candidates and national officials. Management and finance decisions are taken by the Party's National Executive Committee, which meets monthly and comprises elected national officers and representatives of the county organisations.

The annual conference of the SNP is its 'supreme governing body'. The National Council, which meets at least three times a year, is the Party's governing body between conferences. Delegates to the annual conference and National Council are appointed by their branches and constituency associations. Three affiliated organisations—the Federation of Student Nationalists, the Young Scottish Nationalists and the SNP Trade Union Group—are also represented.

Central Offices
Plaid Cymru has a central office with a chief executive and administrative assistant to deal with election organisation, finance and internal administration. The Communications Officer deals with public relations, press work and internal communication.

The headquarters of the SNP comprises five departments: organisation, administration, press, research, and publications.

Party Finance
Three-quarters of Plaid Cymru's total income comes from donations other than those from the constituency parties, and from miscellaneous sources, including the sale of literature.

About two-thirds of the SNP's central income is derived from membership subscriptions; the Party does not publish an annual income figure.

Party Leaders

The leader of Plaid Cymru, known as the president, need not necessarily be an MP. Elections of the president and vice-president take place by ballot held in party branches and area meetings. The election is for a two-year term. The current president of Plaid Cymru is Mr Dafydd Wigley, MP, who was elected in 1991.

In the SNP the offices of leader of the Party in the country and leader of the MPs in the House of Commons may be separate. The leader of the SNP members in the House of Commons is responsible for the day-to-day tactics of the party in Parliament, within the broad policy framework agreed by the party's annual conference. The leader of the Party outside the Commons, however, is the National Convener, who is elected (or re-elected) annually by the party conference. He or she is responsible for the Party's overall organisation. The leader of the SNP in the House of Commons is Mrs Margaret Ewing, MP, elected in 1987, and the National Convener and leader of the Party is Mr Alex Salmond, MP, elected in 1990.

Northern Ireland Parties

Members of Parliament representing Northern Ireland constituencies belong to political parties organised separately from those in the rest of Britain.

There are two major Unionist parties, representing most of the Province's Protestant community, and committed to the maintenance of Northern Ireland's union with Great Britain. The Ulster Unionist Party is the descendant of the party which provided the Government of Northern Ireland from 1921 to 1972 when the Stormont Parliament was prorogued (discontinued without being dissolved) and direct rule from Westminster introduced. The second major Unionist party, the Democratic Unionist Party, was formed in 1971.

The Social Democratic and Labour Party, the main Nationalist party, attracts support from a majority of Northern Ireland's Catholic community and aspires eventually towards a constitutionally achieved united Ireland. The Party was founded in 1970.

Two other parties also attract a substantial amount of support. The Alliance Party, launched in 1970, attracts support from both Unionist and Nationalist communities, but has not been successful in Westminster elections. Sinn Fein, which supports the campaign of the Provisional Irish Republican Army (IRA), a terrorist organisation, held one seat at Westminster from 1983 to 1992, although the holder refused to take it up. The party lost the seat to the SDLP in the 1992 general election.

At the General Election in April 1992 the 17 Northern Ireland seats were distributed as follows: Ulster Unionist 9; Democratic

Unionist 3; Social Democratic and Labour 4; Ulster Popular Unionist 1. The total number of votes gained by the five main political parties in Northern Ireland and their percentage of the total vote in the Province in the 1992 General Election are as shown in Table 3.

Table 3: Northern Ireland Parties

Party	Total votes	Percentage of total NI vote
Ulster Unionist	271,049	34.5
Democratic Unionist	103,039	13.1
Social Democratic and Labour	184,445	23.5
Sinn Fein	78,291	10.0
Alliance	68,665	8.7

Also elected was the Ulster Popular Unionist Sir James Kilfedder, who received 19,305 votes (2.5 per cent); he was the only MP elected without the support of a party machine.

Branches and Constituency Associations

Outside Parliament, the basic units of organisation in the *Ulster Unionist Party* are the local branches, which are based mainly on local government electoral wards. A number of branches together form the local constituency association, which elects its own officers and delegates for the Council and Party Executive, as well as selecting candidates for parliamentary elections.

In the *Democratic Unionist Party* membership of the local branch is open to anyone aged 18 or over who is on the electoral register for the area covered by the branch and who has given a written undertaking to support the constitution and rules of the

Party. Each branch elects its own officers annually and is allowed to decide its own rules, providing these do not conflict with the party constitution and rules. Branches are affiliated to the local constituency association, which meets at least three times a year. Full members elect annually the leading officers of the association and whatever other officers they think appropriate. They also elect four members to represent the constituency on the Central Executive Committee (see p. 46). Each association has a standing committee with overall responsibility for organising and co-ordinating its affairs, subject to the approval of the full association. It includes two representatives elected each year from every local branch within the constituency.

In the *Social Democratic and Labour Party* branches have two classes of membership: individual members and corporate members. Individual members must be attached to the appropriate branch operating in the constituency where they live or where they are registered as electors, and must support the principles and aims of the Party. Corporate members consist of trade unions affiliated to the Irish Congress of Trade Unions, co-operative societies, socialist societies, professional associations and cultural organisations. Branches appoint delegates to the local constituency council which promotes the policies of the Party, co-ordinates the work of the constituency branches, and runs an effective electoral organisation within the constituency. Branches and constituency councils elect their leading officers at an annual general meeting.

Parliamentary Candidates

The selection of prospective parliamentary candidates for the *Ulster Unionist Party* begins with the placing of advertisements in the local press inviting applications. These are normally processed by the local executive or management committee, which may either prepare a shortlist or place all applicants before a selection conference. Candidates have an opportunity to address the selection meeting and to answer questions, and voting continues until one candidate obtains an overall majority.

In the *Democratic Unionist Party* prospective parliamentary candidates are selected by the constituency association, with voting taking place by secret ballot. The names of the selected candidates go before the Central Executive Committee for final confirmation.

In the *Social Democratic and Labour Party* prospective parliamentary candidates are chosen by a selection convention consisting of delegates appointed by branches affiliated to the constituency council, and organised by the Executive Committee. A prospective candidate must be proposed and seconded in writing by individual party members, and the nomination forwarded to the Executive Committee. The candidate is elected by secret ballot, each delegate at the convention having one vote. The Executive Committee has the power to confirm or to refuse to confirm the choice of candidates.

Annual Conferences, Executive Committees and Party Councils

The *Ulster Unionist Party* holds an annual conference organised by the Party's Executive Committee. Constituency associations and affiliated bodies may put forward resolutions for consideration; these then go before the Executive Committee, which may approve, amend or reject them.

The Party Executive comprises between four and six delegates from each constituency association and delegates from affiliated groups, the Women's Unionist Council, the Young Unionists and the Orange Order.

The governing body of the Party is the Ulster Unionist Council, which is responsible for the general organisation and promotion of the Party's affairs, including the annual election of party officers, among them the party leader. As with the Party Executive, the Council's officers are elected annually.

The *Democratic Unionist Party* holds an annual conference which any party member may attend, but at which only delegates may vote. The conference is organised by the Central Executive Committee, and local branches and constituency associations may put forward resolutions which go before the Central Executive Committee for consideration.

The Central Executive Committee controls the day-to-day business of the Party and consists of elected members from each constituency association as well as the party leader and deputy leader. The leading officers of the Committee, who are also officers of the central delegates' assembly are elected annually by secret ballot from among its members.

The central delegates' assembly, which confirms all party manifestos, consists of members elected by and from each local branch.

The supreme governing authority of the *Social Democratic and Labour Party* is the party conference, which decides the Party's policies. It is normally held once a year and is attended by delegates appointed both by branches and by corporate members. Each delegate attending the conference has one vote. The conference elects the leading party officers, including the chairman and two vice-chairmen. Elections are by secret ballot using the single transferable vote system.

The Executive Committee controls the Party's day-to-day organisation. It interprets the Party's constitution and implements conference decisions and develops policy between conferences. The Committee, which meets at least 12 times a year, consists of the party officers and 15 individual members elected at the conference.

There is also a Central Council, which provides a means of communication between the membership and the central organisation of the Party. It meets twice a year and includes branch representatives and representatives from each constituency council and each district executive.

Party Leaders

Until 1974 *Ulster Unionist* MPs took the Conservative Whip in Parliament. However, since the Northern Ireland Parliament was suspended in 1972, Ulster Unionists have operated in Parliament as an independent force. The leader of the Party is elected at the annual general meeting of the Council. James Molyneaux, MP, has been the leader of the Ulster Unionist Party since 1979.

In the *Democratic Unionist Party* the aims of the parliamentary party include providing a means of consultation and action for the Party's MPs, and co-ordinating the efforts of the Party. It elects officers annually from among its membership and fills any other posts it considers necessary. The leader of the Democratic Unionist Party is the Reverend Ian Paisley, MP, elected in 1971.

The leader of the *Social Democratic and Labour Party* has traditionally been elected by the Party's parliamentary group following a General Election. John Hume, MP, has been leader of the party since 1980.

Appendix 1:
Principal Minor Parties

This appendix covers parties which gained approximately 1 per cent of the total vote in the constituencies they contested at the General Election of April 1992.

Co-operative Party

The Co-operative Party was formed in 1917 and its first MP was elected in 1918, joining the Parliamentary Labour Party in the House of Commons. In 1927 the Co-operative Party reached a formal understanding with the Labour Party, and Co-operative Party branches became eligible for affiliation to constituency Labour parties. In 1946 an agreement was reached whereby sponsored Co-operative candidates were to run formally as Co-operative and Labour candidates, and in 1959 it was agreed that the number of Co-operative parliamentary candidates should be limited to 30. In the 1992 General Election the Co-operative Party fielded 21 candidates, 14 of whom were elected as MPs.

Liberal Party

In the 1992 General Election the Liberal Party—comprising Liberal members who opposed the Party's merger with the Social Democratic Party in 1988 (see p. 6)—polled 64,744 votes, an average of 1.7 per cent of the vote.

Green Party
The Green Party (known as the Ecology Party up to 1985) was founded in 1973 after the publication of *Blueprint for Survival*, a work published by the editors of the *Ecologist* magazine, which offered radical solutions to environmental problems.

In the 1992 General Election the Green Party fielded 253 candidates, who together polled 170,368 votes—an average of 1.3 per cent of the vote.

British National Party
Formed in the 1980s, the British National Party polled an average of 1.2 per cent of the vote in the 1992 General Election.

Appendix 2:
General Election Results 1945–92

The following tables show the results of the 14 General Elections held between 1945 and 1992. Redistribution of seats took place in 1950, 1955, 1974 and 1983.

Sources: All figures in the tables below are taken from Butler and Kavanagh: *The British General Election of 1992*; and Butler, D. and G.: *British Political Facts: 1900–1994* (see Further Reading).

Table 4: General Election Result 1945 (5 July)

Party	Votes cast	MPs elected	Candi- dates	% Share of total vote
Labour	11,995,152	393	604	47.8
Conservative	9,988,306	213	624	39.8
Liberal	2,248,226	12	306	9.0
Communist	102,780	2	21	0.4
Common Wealth	110,634	1	23	0.4
Others	640,880	19	104	2.0
Total	25,085,978	640	1,682	100.0

Note: Differences between totals and sums of their component parts are due to rounding.

Electorate 33,240,391 Turnout 72.7%

Table 5: General Election Result 1950 (23 February)

Party	Votes cast	MPs elected	Candi- dates	% Share of total vote
Labour	13,266,592	315	617	46.1
Conservative	12,502,567	298	620	43.5
Liberal	2,621,548	9	475	9.1
Communist	91,746	0	100	0.3
Others	290,218	3	56	1.0
Total	**28,772,671**	**625**	**1,868**	**100.0**

Electorate 33,269,770 Turnout 84.0%

Table 6: General Election Result 1951 (25 October)

Party	Votes cast	MPs elected	Candi- dates	% Share of total vote
Conservative	13,717,538	321	617	48.0
Labour	13,948,605	295	617	48.8
Liberal	730,556	6	109	2.5
Communist	21,640	0	10	0.1
Others	177,329	3	23	0.6
Total	**28,595,668**	**625**	**1,376**	**100.0**

Electorate 34,645,573 Turnout 82.5%

Table 7: General Election Result 1955 (26 May)

Party	Votes cast	MPs elected	Candi- dates	% Share of total vote
Conservative	13,286,569	344	623	49.7
Labour	12,404,970	277	670	46.4
Liberal	722,405	6	110	2.7
Communist	33,144	0	17	0.1
Others	313,410	3	39	1.1
Total	**26,760,498**	**630**	**1,409**	**100.0**

Note: Differences between totals and sums of their component parts are due to rounding.

Electorate 34,858,263 Turnout 76.7%

Table 8: General Election Result 1959 (8 October)

Party	Votes cast	MPs elected	Candi- dates	% Share of total vote
Conservative	13,749,830	365	625	49.4
Labour	12,215,538	258	621	43.8
Liberal	1,638,571	6	216	5.9
Plaid Cymru	77,571	0	20	0.3
Communist	30,897	0	18	0.1
Scottish National	21,738	0	5	0.1
Others	12,464	1	31	0.4
Total	**27,859,241**	**630**	**1,536**	**100.0**

Note: Differences between totals and sums of their component parts are due to rounding.

Electorate 35,397,080 Turnout 78.8%

Table 9: General Election Result 1964 (15 October)

Party	Votes cast	MPs elected	Candi- dates	% Share of total vote
Labour	12,205,814	317	628	44.1
Conservative	12,001,396	304	630	43.4
Liberal	3,092,878	9	365	11.2
Plaid Cymru	69,507	0	23	0.3
Scottish National	64,044	0	15	0.2
Communist	45,932	0	36	0
Others	168,422	0	60	0.6
Total	**27,655,374**	**630**	**1,757**	**100.0**

Note: Differences between totals and sums of their component parts are due to rounding.

Electorate 35,892,572 Turnout 77.1%

Table 10: General Election Result 1966 (31 March)

Party	Votes cast	MPs elected	Candi- dates	% Share of total vote
Labour	13,064,951	363	621	47.9
Conservative	11,418,433	253	629	41.9
Liberal	2,327,533	12	311	8.5
Scottish National	128,474	0	20	0.2
Communist	62,112	0	57	0.2
Plaid Cymru	61,071	0	20	0.2
Others	170,569	2	31	0.6
Total	**27,263,606**	**630**	**1,707**	**100.0**

Note: Differences between totals and sums of their component parts are due to rounding.

Electorate 35,964,684 Turnout 75.8%

Table 11: General Election Result 1970 (18 June)

Party	Votes cast	MPs elected	Candi-dates	% Share of total vote
Conservative	13,145,123	330	628	46.4
Labour	12,179,341	287	624	43.0
Liberal	2,117,035	6	332	7.5
Scottish National	306,802	1	65	1.1
Plaid Cymru	175,016	0	36	0.6
Communist	37,970	0	58	0.1
Others	383,511	6	94	1.4
Total	**28,344,798**	**630**	**1,837**	**100.0**

Note: Differences between totals and sums of their component parts are due to rounding.

Electorate 39,342,013 Turnout 72.0%

Table 12: General Election Result 1974 (28 February)

Party	Votes cast	MPs elected	Candi-dates	% Share of total vote
Labour	11,639,243	301	623	37.1
Conservative	11,868,906	297	623	37.9
Liberal	6,063,470	14	517	19.3
Scottish National	632,032	7	70	2.0
Plaid Cymru	171,364	2	36	0.6
National Front	76,865	0	54	0.3
Communist	32,741	0	44	0.1
Northern Ireland parties	717,986	12	48	2.3
Others	131,059	2	120	0.4
Total	**31,333,226**	**635**	**2,135**	**100.0**

Note: Differences between totals and sums of their component parts are due to rounding.

Electorate 39,798,899 Turnout 78.7%

Table 13: General Election Result 1974 (10 October)

Party	Votes cast	MPs elected	Candi- dates	% Share of total vote
Labour	11,457,079	319	623	39.2
Conservative	10,464,817	277	623	35.8
Liberal	5,346,754	13	619	18.3
Scottish National	839,617	11	71	2.9
Plaid Cymru	166,321	3	36	0.6
National Front	113,843	0	90	0.4
Communist	17,426	0	29	0.1
Northern Ireland parties	702,094	12	43	2.4
Others	81,227	0	118	0.3
Total	**29,189,178**	**635**	**2,252**	**100.0**

Note: Differences between totals and sums of their component parts are due to rounding.

Electorate 40,072,971 Turnout 72.8%

Table 14: General Election Result 1979 (3 May)

Party	Votes cast	MPs elected	Candi- dates	% Share of total vote
Conservative	13,697,690	339	622	43.9
Labour	11,532,148	269	523	36.9
Liberal	4,313,811	11	577	13.8
Scottish National	504,259	2	71	1.6
Plaid Cymru	132,544	2	36	0.4
National Front	190,747	0	303	0.6
Ecology	38,116	0	53	0.1
Communist	15,938	0	38	0.1
Workers Revolutionary	13,535	0	60	0.1
Northern Ireland parties	695,889	12	64	2.2
Others	85,338	0	129	0.3
Total	**31,220,010**	**635**	**2,576**	**100.0**

Note: Differences between totals and sums of their component parts are due to rounding.

Electorate 41,093,264 Turnout 76.0%

Table 15: General Election Result 1983 (9 June)

Party	Votes cast	MPs elected	Candi-dates	% Share of total vote
Conservative	13,012,602	397	633	42.4
Labour	8,457,124	209	633	27.6
Liberal–Social Democratic Alliance[a]	7,780,577	23	633	25.4
Scottish National	331,975	2	72	1.1
Plaid Cymru	125,309	2	38	0.4
Ecology	54,102	0	109	0.2
National Front	27,053	0	60	0.1
British National	14,321	0	53	0.0
Communist	11,596	0	35	0.0
Workers Revolutionary	3,800	0	21	0.0
Northern Ireland parties[b]	763,474	17	94	2.5
Others	87,962	0	198	0.3
Total	**30,669,895**	**650**	**2,579**	**100.0**

Note: Differences between totals and sums of their component parts are due to rounding.

Electorate 42,197,344 Turnout 72.7%

[a] Seventeen Liberal members were elected out of 322 candidates, and six SDP members out of 311 candidates.

[b] All figures exclude the Ecology Party candidate in Antrim N., who is included in the Ecology figures.

Table 16: General Election Result 1987 (11 June)

Party	Votes cast	MPs elected	Candi-dates	% Share of total vote
Conservative[a]	13,763,066	376	633	42.3
Labour	10,029,944	229	633	30.8
Liberal–Social Democratic Alliance[b]	7,341,152	22	633	22.6
Scottish National	416,873	3	71	1.3
Plaid Cymru	123,589	3	38	0.4
Green	89,753	0	134	0.3
Communist	6,078	0	19	0.0
Northern Ireland parties	730,152	17	77	2.5
Others	32,463	0	87	0.1
Total	**32,536,137**	**650**	**2,325**	**100.0**

Note: Differences between totals and the sums of their component parts are due to rounding.

Electorate 43,181,321 Turnout 75.3%

[a] These figures include the Speaker of the House of Commons, who stood as 'Mr Speaker seeking re-election'. He was, before his election as Speaker, a Conservative member.

[b] Seventeen Liberal members were elected out of 327 candidates, and five SDP members out of 306 candidates.

For results of the 1992 General Election see p. 13.

State of the Parties in the House of Commons in early March 1994

As a result of by-elections since the 1992 General Election, the distribution of seats in the House of Commons in early March 1994 was: Conservative 330, Labour 266, Liberal Democrats 22, Plaid Cymru 4, Scottish National 3, Ulster Unionist 9, Democratic Unionist 3, Ulster Popular Unionist 1, Social Democratic and Labour 4, Mr R. Allason (from whom the Conservative whip has been temporarily withdrawn) 1, and vacant 4. Not included are the Speaker and her three deputies (the Chairman of Ways and Means and the first and second Deputy Chairman of Ways and Means) who do not vote except in their official capacity in the event of a tie.

Party Addresses

The following are the addresses of parties referred to in this book:

Conservative and Unionist Party, 32 Smith Square, London SW1P 3HH.

Labour Party, 144–152 Walworth Road, London SE17 1JT.

Liberal Democrats, 4 Cowley Street, London SW1P 3NB.

Scottish Liberal Democrats, 4 Clifton Terrace, Edinburgh EH12 5DR.

Welsh Liberal Democrats, 57 St Mary's Street, Cardiff CF1 IFE.

Plaid Cymru, 51 Cathedral Road, Cardiff CF1 9HD.

Scottish National Party, 6 North Charlotte Street, Edinburgh EH2 4JH.

Ulster Unionist Party, 3 Glengall Street, Belfast BT12 5AE.

Democratic Unionist Party, 296 Albertbridge Road, Belfast BT5 4GX.

Social Democratic and Labour Party, 24 Mount Charles, Botanic Avenue, Belfast BT7 1NZ.

Liberal Party, 1a Pine Grove, Southport, Lancs PR5 9AQ.

Sinn Fein, 44 Parnell Square, Dublin 1.

Alliance Party, 88 University Street, Belfast BT7 1HE.

Co-operative Party, 342 Hoe Street, London E17 9PX.

Green Party, 10 Station Parade, Balham High Road, London SW12 9AZ.

British National Party, 154 Upper Wickham Lane, Welling, Kent DA16 3DX.

Further Reading

Britain: A One Party State? Alderman, G.
and Blake, Robert [Lord].   Christopher Helm 1989

The British General Election of 1992.
Butler, David and Kavanagh, Denis.   Macmillan 1992

The British Party System. Ingle, Stephen.   Blackwell 1989

British Political Facts: 1900–1994.
Butler, David and Butler, Gareth.   Macmillan 1994

The Changing Labour Party.
Smith, M.J. and Spear, J. (eds.)   Routledge 1992

The Conservative Party from Peel to Thatcher.
Bogdanor, Vernon.   Methuen 1985

Governing Without a Majority.
Butler, David.   Macmillan 1986

*Multi-Party Politics and
the Constitution.*   Cambridge University Press 1983

The Politics of the Labour Party.
Kavanagh, D. (ed.)   Allen and Unwin 1982

Selecting the Party Leader: Britain in Comparative Perspective.
Punnett, R.M.   Harvester Wheatsheaf 1992

A Short History of the Liberal Party 1900–1992.
Cook, Chris.   Macmillan 1993

Third Party Politics Since 1945: Liberals, Alliance and Liberal Democrats. Stevenson, J. Blackwell 1992

Times Guide to the House of Commons. April 1992. Times Books 1992

United Kingdom Political Parties since 1945. Seldon, A (ed.). Philip Allen 1990

Other titles in the Aspects of Britain series:

Parliament	HMSO	1994
Parliamentary Elections	HMSO	1991
The Monarchy	HMSO	1991
The British System of Government	HMSO	1994
History and Functions of Government Departments	HMSO	1993
The Civil Service	HMSO	1994
Britain's Legal Systems	HMSO	1993
Pressure Groups	HMSO	1994

Index

Printed in the UK for HMSO.
Dd 0297868, 6/94, C30, 56-6734, 5673.

024026